BELMONT
THE RIDGEWAY, MILL HILL

LIBRARY & MEDIA
RESOURCE CENTRE
Telephone 020 8959 1431

weblinks

You don't need a computer to use this book. But, for readers who do have access to the Internet, the book provides links to recommended websites which offer additional information and resources on the subject.

You will find weblinks boxes like this on some pages of the book.

---
weblinks

For more information about David Beckham, go to www.waylinks.co.uk /21CentLives/Sport

---

waylinks.co.uk

To help you find the recommended websites easily and quickly, weblinks are provided on our own website, **waylinks.co.uk.** These take you straight to the relevant websites and save you typing in the Internet address yourself.

Internet safety

↗ Never give out personal details, which include: your name, address, school, telephone number, email address, password and mobile number.

↗ Do not respond to messages which make you feel uncomfortable – tell an adult.

↗ Do not arrange to meet in person someone you have met on the Internet.

↗ Never send your picture or anything else to an online friend without a parent's or teacher's permission.

↗ If you see anything that worries you, tell an adult.

A note to adults
Internet use by children should be supervised. We recommend that you install filtering software which blocks unsuitable material.

Website content

The weblinks for this book are checked and updated regularly. However, because of the nature of the Internet, the content of a website may change at any time, or a website may close down without notice. While the Publishers regret any inconvenience this may cause readers, they cannot be responsible for the content of any website other than their own.

HODDER
Wayland

21st CENTURY LIVES
SPORTS PEOPLE

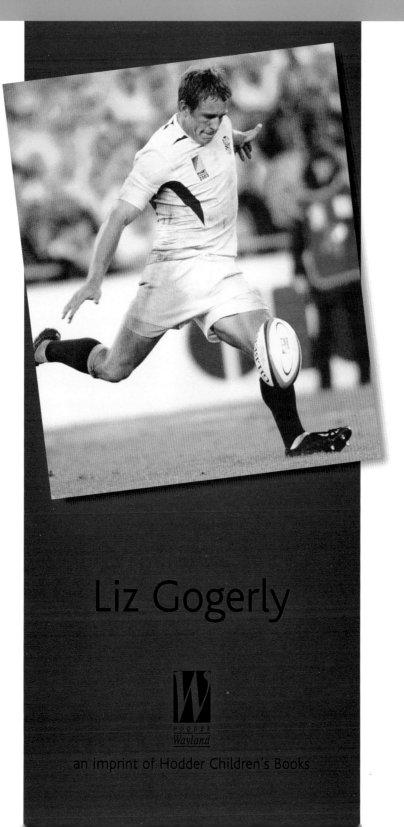

Liz Gogerly

HODDER
Wayland

an imprint of Hodder Children's Books

Editor: Hayley Leach
Design: Peter Bailey for Proof Books
Cover design: Hodder Children's Books

Published in Great Britain in 2004 by Hodder Wayland,
an imprint of Hodder Children's Books.

British Library Cataloguing in Publication Data
Sports people. – (21st century lives)
1. Athletes – Biography – Juvenile literature
I. Title
796'.0922

ISBN: 0750245972

Cover: World Cup 2002 Denmark vs England. David Beckham celebrates
victory over Denmark.

Picture acknowledgements: Cover Tim De Waele/Corbis; 4 Zuma
Archive/ZUMA/Corbis; 5 Tim De Waele/Corbis; 6 Simon Bruty/SI/NewSport/Corbis;
7 Michael Kim/Corbis; 8 Manuel Blondeau/Photo & Co./Corbis; Title page and 9 Nick
Laham/Getty Images; 10 Duomo/Corbis; 11 Susan Mullane/NewSport/Corbis;12 Gary
Newkirk/NewSport/Corbis; 13 Duomo/Corbis; 14 G. Lagaced/Corbis Sygma; 15
Mousis Francois/Corbis Sygma; 16 Mike Hewitt/Getty Images; 17 Hamish Blair/Getty
Images; 18 Rune Hellestad/Corbis; 19 Michael Steele/Getty Images; 20 Alex
Livesey/Getty Images; 21 Alain Issock/Corbis

Printed in China by WKT Company Ltd

Hodder Children's Books
a division of Hodder Headline Limited
338 Euston Road
London NW1 3BH

Contents

David Beckham

Beckham and his wife, Victoria

" **All I ever wanted to do was kick a football about. It didn't enter my head to do anything else. I think I was programmed by my dad to some extent. I knew he wanted me to be a footballer and he encouraged me to play when I was a kid. I enjoyed playing, whether it was in the garden or on a pitch with the Sunday league team.** "
David Beckham

Beckham: My World **by David Beckham**
(Hodder and Stoughton, 2000)

Name: David Robert Beckham

Nickname: Becks

Date and place of birth: 2 May 1975, Leytonstone, London

Training: As a schoolboy David trained with his father and at London club, Tottenham Hotspur. At 16 he signed as a trainee for Manchester United.

Football teams played for:
Beckham made his league debut in 1995, aged 19, for the Manchester United reserves. He played for England for the first time in 1996. Beckham remained with the 'Red Devils' until 2003 when he transferred to top Spanish club Real Madrid.

Major achievements: Being made captain of the England team. One of his finest moments was scoring in the 93rd minute of the World Cup qualifying match with Greece. It was this winning goal that ensured England reached the 2002 World Cup.

Sponsorship: Adidas and Pepsi. These days he is so popular in the Far East that over half of his corporate sponsors are based in the Asia-Pacific region.

Something you might not know about him: He supports the charity the National Society for the Prevention of Cruelty to Children (NSPCC). He makes surprise visits to ill children and gives them free tickets for a match.

Become a pro! To 'bend it like Beckham' you need dedication. Scoring so many long-range goals and penalties isn't luck, it takes hours of practice each day. Beckham is also a terrific team player, well known for his brilliant passing skills and excellent free kicks.

While other teenagers were going out with their friends, David Beckham was living, breathing and dreaming football. His ultimate wish was to play for Manchester United. When he left school at 16 his dream came true and he was signed as a Man United trainee. In 1992 he made his first-team debut but he had to wait until 1995 to become the regular right midfielder.

In his first season David scored some startling goals but it was the 1996-1997 season when things really started to happen for him. He achieved star status when he scored from the halfway line against Wimbledon. At the same time he began dating Victoria Adams from the Spice Girls. The 'beautiful' young couple were rarely out of the tabloid press. As David's talent on the pitch grew, so did his reputation for dressing in fashionable clothes and enjoying a celebrity lifestyle.

It seemed like David could do no wrong. In 1996 he made his debut for England, but in the 1998 World Cup campaign disaster struck. During the match against Argentina David was sent off for kicking Diego Simeone. This left the England team one man down and many fans blamed David for England being knocked out of the Cup.

On a personal level 1999 was a better year. His first son Brooklyn was born and shortly afterwards David and Victoria were married. Family life seemed to mature David and in 2000 he was appointed captain of the England squad. In the 2002 World Cup he was outstanding on the pitch and was a strong team leader. In the same year he became a father once again to baby Romeo.

David often makes front-page news. In 2003 the main story was about his troubled relationship with Man United manager, Sir Alex Ferguson. That year he finally did the unthinkable: he left United and signed a four-year contract with Real Madrid. Though he now lives in Spain David is as popular at home as he has ever been and in November 2003 he was presented with a special award called an OBE (Officer of the Order of the British Empire) by the Queen.

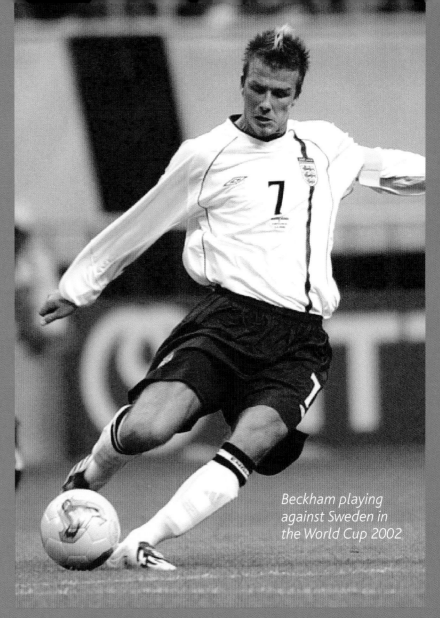

Beckham playing against Sweden in the World Cup 2002

"Beckham has won everyone's respect. We knew he was a good player but we didn't expect him to be so influential... We are very impressed with him, with the way he runs for everything and tries his best. At Real there is always room for another big-name player."

Ronaldo, Beckham's team-mate at Real Madrid, October 2003.

weblinks

For more information about David Beckham, go to
www.waylinks.co.uk/21CentLives/Sport

Michael Schumacher

Formula One Champion

Michael Schumacher

Name: Michael Schumacher

Nickname: Schumi or Schuey

Date and place of birth: 3 January 1969, Hürth-Hermülheim, Germany

Training: Michael began his racing career in karting, winning the German Junior Kart Championship when he was just 13. He moved into the fast lane in 1990 when he began sports car racing. His debut in Formula One racing came in 1991 at the Belgian Grand Prix.

Formula One teams driven for: Jordan (1991), Benetton (1992-1995), Ferrari (1996-present)

Major achievements: Winning the Formula One World Championship in 1994 when he was 26, then taking the title again in 1995, 2000, 2001, 2002 and 2003.

Something you might not know about him: Michael is extremely fit. A friend once said that when Michael takes his dog for a walk it's the dog that gets tired first! He also enjoys playing soccer and tennis, and he is an excellent swimmer and skier.

Become a pro! To become World Champion takes fitness, intelligence, concentration and the ability to stay calm when you are under pressure. Michael stands out because he drives at his maximum speed very early in a race. He says that he has learned 95 per cent of the circuit by the end of the first few laps. Other drivers, he claims, do not feel as confident as quickly and this gives him an advantage.

> "Hero status makes me uncomfortable. I don't want it, I have a problem with it, just as I do with the hysteria surrounding my person. Obviously I appreciate what people think of my achievements and how it lifts them but I don't see myself as a hero."
> Michael Schumacher

Schumacher: The Official Inside Story of the Formula One Icon by Sabine Kehm
(Ebury Press, 2003)

Michael Schumacher being chased by his brother Ralf during the Canadian Grand Prix 2003

In October 2003 the German Formula One star Michael Schumacher won the World Championship for a record sixth time. He also became the first person to win the Championship four years in a row, making him the most successful driver in the 54-year history of Formula One.

Fast vehicles and racing have been in Michael Schumacher's blood since he was a young boy. The fascination with speed began at four years old when his father, a builder, made him a go-kart. From then onwards his parents encouraged their eldest son to race. They enrolled him at his local kart club and at 14 their shy but determined son scooped first place in the Junior Kart Championship of 1984-1985.

By 1989 Michael had caught the eye of Willi Weber, a German businessman. He backed Michael in the 1989 and 1990 Formula Three Championships. In 1991 Michael raced for the Mercedes-Benz sportscar racing team. Once again Michael's skill was noted, and he was poached by the Jordan racing team. That year he made his debut in Formula One racing at the Belgian Grand Prix.

In 1992 Michael moved to the Benetton racing team, winning his first Formula One Championship in 1994. Unfortunately, his early win was clouded by allegations of cheating. It was suggested that he deliberately rammed his rival, the English driver Damon Hill. The 1995 season saw many scrapes between Michael and Damon Hill but Michael went on to win his second Championship. That same year Michael married Corinna Betsch. Today, Michael is very much a family man. He has two young children who he tries to protect from too much publicity. Not that keeping out of the spotlight is easy for the World Champion. In 1996 he moved to Ferrari for an estimated salary of $30 million. Whenever Michael races he wows the crowds with his nerves of steel.

'I am not really afraid for Michael… I have absolute faith in him, in his strength, his judgement, his temperament. Michael will always be a dogged fighter, battling to the end, but he is not a gambler. He never takes unnecessary risks. He is much too sensible for that. He knows when there's no longer any point in taking someone on, he simply waits and mounts an attack later.'

Michael's wife Corinna Schumacher on her husband's racing skills
Schumacher: The Official Inside Story of the Formula One Icon by Sabine Kehm
(Ebury Press, 2003)

weblinks

For more information about Michael Schumacher, go to
www.waylinks.co.uk/21CentLives/Sport

Jonny Wilkinson
Rugby Hero

Jonny Wilkinson celebrating with his team mates after winning the Rugby World Cup 2003

" I do have a fear of failure, so I do need to go through my drills so that I know that, when I step up to a kick, I have done it many times over in training... I want people to put me up there with the best that there has been. It would be a waste if, when you hung up your boots, it was finished, that was it, nobody ever mentioned you again. I don't think I could live with the feeling of regret if I don't make the most of what I've got now. "
Jonny Wilkinson

The *Daily Telegraph*, November 24 2003

Name: Jonny Peter Wilkinson

Nickname: Wilko

Date and place of birth: 25 May 1979, Surrey, England

Training: Jonny played rugby for his schools, as well as cricket and tennis.

Teams played for: He joined the Newcastle Falcons in 1997 and made his debut for England in 1998.

Major achievements: Scoring the triumphant drop-goal in the last minute of extra-time in the match against Australia, clinching the 2003 World Cup for the England team.

Something you might not know about him: Jonny does not like to drink alcohol. When the rest of the World Cup squad were celebrating the win in Australia in 2003 Jonny hardly touched a drop.

Secret of Success: When Jonny is in front of the posts all he is really thinking about is Doris. Doris is a fictional character that Jonny's coach made-up to help Jonny aim the ball. He imagines a woman sitting between the posts, about 20 seats up, and trys to aim the ball directly at her. So when Jonny is having trouble with his kicking practice he trys to 'hit a few Dorises'.

Become a pro! Jonny is always first and last off the training field. Often he is on the pitch practising his kicking 90 minutes before the other players turn up. He does not stop until he is confident that he can kick the ball from every angle. It is only by practising so hard that he can satisfy himself that there will be no 'what ifs' and 'if onlys' when he is playing an important match.

Jonny kicks the winning drop-goal during the Rugby World Cup final against Australia in 2003

At the age of 18 Jonny became the youngest player ever for England. In 1998 he made his debut against Ireland and was chosen for the summer tour of Australia. Back at Newcastle he became the permanent number 10 player and goal kicker. Since that time Jonny has earned the admiration and respect of his Newcastle and England team players and fans. At 21 he was already in the record books, becoming England's leading point scorer of all time. By the year 2003, especially after his magnificent performance at the World Cup, many fans hailed him as the best rugby player in the world. He was awarded an MBE (Member of the Order of the British Empire) in 2003 and an OBE (Officer of the Order of the British Empire) in 2004 for his service to English rugby.

What is the secret of Jonny's success? Some say he has turned kicking into a science. His look of concentration and the way in which he holds his hands as he takes a kick is all part of his individual style. He is also fast and explosive on the pitch, and a mean tackler. Jonny is far more modest about his skills. He claims he is a team player and believes that he can only do his job when everybody else in the squad pulls together. He is also dedicated to rugby, often citing his ten-year pact with himself to sacrifice everything for the sake of the game.

Newspapers rang with headlines like 'King of the World' and 'Jonny B Good' after the 2003 Rugby World Cup final in Sydney, Australia. Overnight, Jonny's last-minute drop goal had turned him into a sporting legend.

Rugby has been part of Jonny Wilkinson's life since he was a young boy. Growing up in Surrey, he was playing rugby from the age of four with his father and older brother. At school Jonny was a good all-round pupil, gaining three A Level passes and a place at Durham University. However, throughout his school days rugby was Jonny's greatest passion. In 1997 he made his mark in the English 18s Schools' Tour of Australia. Soon afterwards he was persuaded to turn down his place at university and sign for the Newcastle Falcons team.

"He's the man with the golden boot and the golden hair. Everything is golden for Jonny."

The public relations guru Max Clifford talking about Jonny Wilkinson after the World Cup 2003
The *Daily Telegraph*, November 24 2003

weblinks

For more information about Jonny Wilkinson, go to
www.waylinks.co.uk/21CentLives/Sport

Serena Williams
Tennis Superstar

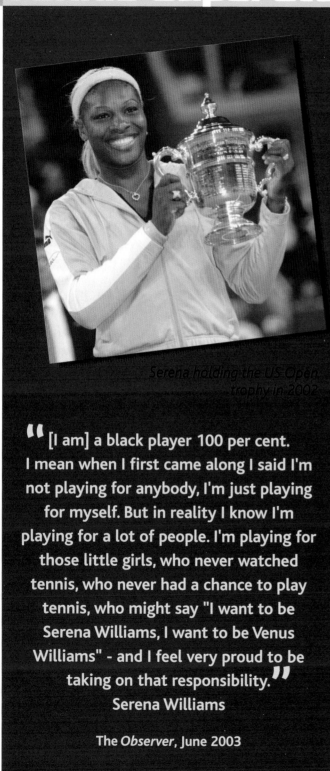

Serena holding the US Open trophy in 2002

"[I am] a black player 100 per cent. I mean when I first came along I said I'm not playing for anybody, I'm just playing for myself. But in reality I know I'm playing for a lot of people. I'm playing for those little girls, who never watched tennis, who never had a chance to play tennis, who might say "I want to be Serena Williams, I want to be Venus Williams" - and I feel very proud to be taking on that responsibility."
Serena Williams

The *Observer*, June 2003

Name: Serena Williams.

Date and place of birth:
26 September 1981, Saginaw, Michigan, USA

Training: Her father, Richard Williams, coaches Serena and her sister, Venus, himself. For many years they practised on the public tennis courts in Compton, a rough, tough suburb of Los Angeles. Serena entered her first tournament at the age of four and a half. Over the next five years, according to her father, Serena won 46 tournaments out of 49. She was ranked the number one player under 12 in southern California. Before she was even a teenager Serena had attracted national attention. The girls attended Ric Macci's Tennis Academy in Florida for a short while in 1991 before their father took up their coaching again.

Major achievements: 'The Serena Slam'! In 2002/03 Serena held four major titles. She won the French Open, Wimbledon, the US Open and the Australian Open and was ranked as the number one female player by the World Tennis Association (WTA).

Something you might not know about her: Even though she is at the peak of her tennis career Serena is already thinking about what she would like to do in the future. She claims that she would like to be an actress. In 2003 she made her first appearance in an American television series called *Street Time*.

Become a pro! It takes talent and determination to become a tennis pro. Serena has had more obstacles than most players have. Since she turned professional in 1995 she has experienced prejudice because of her race and background. Even though Serena is an incredible tennis player it is her confidence and attitude that has got her to the top.

Venus and Serena Williams have dominated women's tennis since the late 1990s. By 2003 a string of victories saw Serena become the number one female tennis player in the world.

Serena's rise to the top reads like a fairytale. The youngest of five girls, she was raised in a violent area of Los Angeles called Compton. Her father, Richard Williams, was determined that his youngest daughters, Venus and Serena, would become top tennis players and he proceeded to teach them himself. The odds were stacked against the Williams sisters from the start. Often their father had to read up on technique so he could show the girls how to play. During one practice session on the public courts they had to duck to avoid bullets from a drive-by shooting.

Serena entered her first tournament when she was four and a half. Even as a young girl her extraordinary talent was noticed by the American press and she was tipped for future success. She turned professional in 1995 and along with her sister quickly became one of the top ranked tennis players in the world. For many years Venus was the better player but in 1999 Serena stepped out from under her sister's shadow to win the US Open, becoming the first sister to win a Grand Slam title.

The next few years seemed to belong to Venus. In 2000 and 2001 Serena had to bow out gracefully as she watched her sister win Wimbledon and the US Open. While Venus hit her winning streak we can only imagine how Serena felt. It certainly seemed to concentrate her game and in 2002 Serena won the French Open, Wimbledon and the US Open. In 2003 she beat her sister in an emotional final at Wimbledon.

Known for her colourful tennis dresses and her huge power game, Serena has brought glamour and strength to female tennis and she's expected to stay at the top of the game for many years to come.

Serena playing in the final at Wimbledon 2002

"...when the Williams sisters have passed into history, no doubt we shall look back in wonder and admiration, and talk long into the night about the extraordinary years in which they had no one to fight but each other."

The *Guardian*, 7 July 2003

weblinks

For more information about Serena Williams, go to
www.waylinks.co.uk/21CentLives/Sport

Tiger Woods
Golfing Genius

Tiger Woods

" It is amazing how much you can learn when you truly enjoy doing something. Golf for me has always been a labor [sic] of love and pleasure, although sometimes impatience got the better of me. Every time that happened, Pop [his father] would remind me how important it is to prepare for life's challenges so that I could face them confidently. He would use golf to teach me about patience, integrity, honesty and humility. **"**
Tiger Woods

Training a Tiger: The Official Book on How to be the Best by Earl Woods
(Hodder and Stoughton, 1998)

Name: Eldrick Woods

Nickname: Tiger (named after a friend of his father's who was also nicknamed Tiger)

Date and place of birth: 30 December 1975, Long Beach, California, USA

Training: Tiger was taught to play golf by his father, Earl Woods. At ten months old Earl Woods took Tiger out of his high chair and let him come over and play with him. Tiger picked up a putter, put a golf ball down and hit the ball straight into the net. Earl Woods called in a professional coach when Tiger was four years old because he felt he had taught Tiger everything he knew.

Major achievements: Tiger keeps breaking all the records! He won the US Junior Amateur Championships three times, becoming the first person to win it more than once. In 2000 he won the Masters, the US Open and the British Open, becoming only the fifth player, and the youngest, to complete the Grand Slam. He is also the first African American or Asian American player to win a major championship.

Something you might not know about him: Tiger is good friends with the famous American basketball player Michael Jordan. The men share a love of golf and both of them have to deal with the pressures associated with sudden fame and wealth. Tiger says that Michael is like his big brother and Michael calls Tiger his hero.

Become a pro! Begin playing golf at an early age. Tiger was on the driving range by the time he was 18 months old, copying his father's swing. Tiger manages to stay on top by practising hard and focusing on winning. When he plays he likes to stay 'in the zone', which means not allowing anything to rattle his nerve or distract him from the game.

Tiger Woods has often been hailed as the greatest living sportsman. Since turning professional in 1996 he has dominated the game of golf, breaking countless records and winning over 50 tournaments.

Encouraged by his father, an ex-lieutenant colonel in the US Army, Tiger was hitting golf balls when he was less than a year old. Earl Woods was determined that his son would become a top golf player and began taking him to the driving range from the age of 18 months. At two, Tiger played golf with the famous comedian Bob Hope on American television. The following year he could shoot 48 for nine holes, the average score of half of the world's club golfers. Tiger followed up this early promise by becoming the youngest US Junior Amateur Champion in golfing history when he was just 15.

Tiger turned professional in 1996 and in the following year, at the age of 21, he became the youngest winner of the US Masters tournament at Augusta in 63 years. He did this with a record margin, in the lowest number of shots. In the same year he won three events on the PGA Tour and was ranked world number one. This was just the beginning of an amazing run of wins, including the British Open (2000), the US Open (2000), the United States PGA Championship (1999, 2000) and the US Masters (2001, 2002).

The secret of Tiger's success is practise, which means going on the course at dawn and spending four hours in one stretch practising his putts. It also means re-inventing and perfecting his strokes and lifting weights in the gym. Ultimately, Tiger has an inner drive to be the best player in the world.

Tiger has made millions of dollars playing golf but he has also done much to enrich the game. His down-to-earth attitude has changed the image of a game that was once white and middle-class. At the same time his youth and mixed-race has made him an inspiration to young people from many backgrounds.

Tiger during the third round of the US Open 2002. He went on to win the tournament.

"I admire [Tiger] for what he's done thus far because for so long it was truly a game that a lot of minorities couldn't play... so in that sense he's carrying an extra burden along with him, to succeed and expand across all racial barriers."
The basketball star Michael Jordan

Tiger Woods: The Making of a Champion
by Tim Rosaforte (Simon and Schuster, 1998)

weblinks

For more information about Tiger Woods, go to
www.waylinks.co.uk/21CentLives/Sport

Ellen MacArthur
Inspirational Yachtswoman

" I have spent my life dreaming of the ocean, since 1994 I have done nothing but sail. It is my passion, my life, and undoubtedly my future...
The Route du Rhum was a demanding race, both the conditions and the boat made it very testing, but it became the most incredible proving ground... I had sailed the boat very little before the start, was learning the whole time, despite getting thrown around somewhat. I never felt out of my depth. I am a tough cookie, not someone who gives up. That is why I am ocean racing alone at 22. **"**
Ellen MacArthur

Taking on the World by Ellen MacArthur
(Michael Joseph, 2002)

Name: Ellen MacArthur

Date and place of birth: 8 July 1976, Derbyshire, UK

Training: Ellen grew-up in Derbyshire, which is nowhere near the sea! She never belonged to any yachting clubs. It was only after a sailing trip with her aunt, at the age of eight, that Ellen was hooked. She spent hours in the school library after that finding out all about sailing. By the time she was 18 she had decided to become a professional sailor.

Major achievements: At 18 Ellen sailed around Britain single-handed. In 2000 she finished second in the Vendée Globe round-the-world event, becoming the youngest woman to sail around the world, and only the second person at that time to sail the globe solo in less than 100 days. In 2002 she finished first in the Route Du Rhum race, becoming the first woman to do so.

Something you might not know about her: Ellen's greatest inspiration is her grandmother, Irene Lewis. She left Ellen money in her will to pay the entrance fee for the Vendée Globe event. Ellen has also inherited her grandmother's determination and spirit. Irene graduated with a degree in European languages from Derby University at the age of 82, three months before her death from lung cancer.

Become a pro! To become a top yachtsperson takes courage and determination. Ellen says there is a 'sailor's self-preservation system' which helps you to forget the bad things that happen and makes you keep going. Being alone for 100 days at sea also means you have to be good at many different things — as well as being skipper on your own boat you need to be an electrician, engineer, sail-maker and doctor so you can cope with any emergency that might arise.

Ellen training on-board the Kingfisher

As a young girl growing up in Derbyshire, Ellen MacArthur loved reading the stories by Arthur Ransome, especially *Swallows and Amazons*. His books were good because the children in them loved to sail. Ellen first took to the sea when she was eight, on family sailing trips. Very soon she was saving her school dinner money to buy her first boat. At 18 Ellen sailed single-handed around the coast of Britain. It was her first adventure at sea alone and Ellen won the Young Sailor of the Year award.

In 1997 Ellen took to the high seas again, this time in her first transatlantic race. She eventually made the crossing in 33 days. The following year she took part in the famous transatlantic race the Route Du Rhum and came first in her class. That year she was voted Yachtsman of the Year in the UK and was given the 'Sailing's Young Hope' award in France.

It was in 2000 that Ellen faced her greatest challenge yet when she took part in the famous round-the-world race, the Vendée Globe. Facing storms and terrifying hurricanes, Ellen risked her life every day. In her 100 days sailing solo she averaged 20-minutes of sleep at a time and survived on mainly freeze-dried food. Ellen came second in the race and became the fastest woman around the world. The following year she received a special award from the Queen called an MBE (Member of the Order of the British Empire).

Ellen has gone on to win other races but in 2003 she had to admit defeat when she attempted to break the Jules Verne round-the-world record. Unfortunately, the mast of her catamaran, Kingfisher 2, was damaged and she had to bow out of the race. She was disappointed to be out of the competition but she didn't let it stop her from racing. In June 2004 Ellen just missed out on breaking a new record for the west-to-east solo transatlantic crossing. The ultimate goal for Ellen is to break the solo round-the-world record, something she is determined to do.

> "I've always loved the sea and the sea has always been a great inspiration to me – seeing the things that other people have done, dreaming about going out on it. That's the reason for being on the water, and I'm a very competitive person, which is the reason for racing."
> Ellen MacArthur
>
> The *Guardian*, January 2002

weblinks

For more information about Ellen MacArthur, go to
www.waylinks.co.uk/21CentLives/Sport

Sachin Tendulkar
Cricket's Superhero

Sachin Tendulkar

"One simple thing is that every time you go out you want to score runs and win matches for India and give your best. It goes without saying and that is my goal – that every innings I play, I play with 100 per cent concentration and dedication, and whatever I achieve it happens during that process. The idea is that every time I go out, I want to score runs and win matches for India."
Sachin talking about his aims when he plays cricket

STAR Sports, March 2002

Name: Sachin Ramesh Tendulkar

Date and place of birth: 24 April 1973, Bombay (now Mumbai), Maharashtra, India

Teams played for: Mumbai, Yorkshire, India

Major achievements: Sachin is recognised as one of the best batsmen in the history of cricket. He has broken many Test Match records. By the time he was 21 he had already made seven centuries in Test cricket, becoming the only batsman ever to do so. In 2002, at the age of 29, Sachin became the youngest cricketer to play 100 Test Match games.

Something you might not know about him: Sachin is a practising Hindu and tries to visit the temple late each night. He is also extremely proud to be Indian and was the first Indian player to wear a sticker with the Indian national flag on his helmet. He also makes sure that he always carries the Indian flag in his kit bag.

Inspiration: Sachin has said that his family is his greatest inspiration. His older brother Agit recognised that young Sachin had a talent for cricket. Agit has been a major influence throughout Sachin's career, as a brother, friend and even a coach.

Become a pro! Sachin is an attacking player who is willing to take chances when he is batting. His best advice for anybody who wants to play top cricket is to follow his or her own style and not to try and copy him. He thinks everyone has their own method of playing cricket and there is no magic recipe for becoming a pro. Sachin puts his own success down to hard work and dedication, as well as opportunity and destiny.

Sachin Tendulkar is a huge hero in his native India and can hardly leave his home for being stampeded by fans. In the world of cricket he is recognised as one of the best ever batsmen of all time. Despite his fame he is a quiet, modest man who has brought his own brand of intelligence to the game of cricket.

Sachin was born in Bombay (now Mumbai), India in 1973. Like many Indian boys he was brought up playing sport, especially cricket which he played with his older brother. Even so, young Sachin was often in trouble with his father, a university professor and poet, for his boyish pranks. In the mid-eighties his family sent him to live with his uncle and auntie in north-east Bombay to be near a new school. The school was famous for its cricket team so Sachin was able to develop his talents. His relatives also happened to live close to Shivaji Park, a massive recreational ground where hundreds of boys gather to play cricket. When he wasn't at school Sachin could usually be found at the ground playing cricket or table tennis.

At 15 Sachin scored a century when he made his debut for Bombay in first-class cricket. The following year he was chosen to play for the Indian cricket team. He made his debut in Test cricket against Pakistan. For the first time he was up against fast-bowlers like Wasim Akram and Waqar Younis. He found the experience rather frightening and didn't expect to be selected for the first team again. Sachin has gone on to captain India, and become the first batsman to score 50 centuries (100 runs) in international cricket. In the 2003 Cricket World Cup he chalked up an impressive 669 runs over ten matches, a new World Cup record, and he earned himself the Man of the Tournament award.

Sachin bats for India during a One Day International against Australia in January 2004

"India are not a one-man team but they are sure as hell a better side when Sachin Tendulkar bats well! He is the focus of attention by the opposition bowlers and so good that even when Ganguly and Azza [fellow team mates] went cheaply he took the pressure on his shoulders and batted like a man inspired. I don't think he is just a great batsman, now he is streets ahead of any player in the world."
Geoffrey Boycott

weblinks

For more information about Sachin Tendulkar, go to
www.waylinks.co.uk/21CentLives/Sport

Paula Radcliffe
Record-breaking Runner

> **"None of us likes to say we have reached our best. None of us likes to say we cannot run faster."**
> **Paula Radcliffe**
>
> The *Scotsman*, 14 April 2003

Name: Paula Jane Radcliffe

Date and place of birth: 17 December 1973, Northwich, Cheshire, UK

Event: Long distance runner

Club: Bedford and County Athletics Club

Training: At nine years old Paula joined the Bedford Athletics Club and was taught by the man who is still her coach, Alex Stanton.

Major achievements: Paula's world-record breaking success began when she ran her first marathon in London in 2002. Paula won the race easily, breaking the record for the fastest ever debut marathon run for a woman. Later that year she ran 1 minute 29 seconds off the world record at the Chicago Marathon. In 2003 she ran a further 1 minute 53 seconds off the world record at the London Marathon.

Something you might not know about her: Paula is against athletes taking performance-enhancing drugs. To make her point Paula insists that she be regularly tested for drugs. At the World Championships in Edmonton in 2001 she demonstrated against a fellow athlete who had tested positive for drugs but had been allowed to run.

Become a pro! As a girl Paula once finished 299th in a cross-country school championship. Paula has never let defeat get her down, and it has taken guts and determination to become a world record holder. Now Paula trains almost every day, running over 140 miles a week. She finishes each training session with a bath of ice cubes, which helps her muscles to recover more quickly.

Running was in Paula's blood from an early age. As a girl of seven she regularly joined her father as he trained to run marathons. Later, the family moved to Bedford where Paula enjoyed running in the surrounding countryside. At school she enjoyed cross-country running, and at nine she joined the local athletics club. Athletics was an important part of Paula's life. She went on to study at Loughborough University where she graduated with a first class honours degree in European Studies. As well as being a record-breaking sportswoman Paula is fluent in French and German.

While she was still at university Paula broke into international athletics. She first caught the public eye when she came fifth in the 5,000 metre final at the 1995 World Championships in Gothenburg. Though Paula went on to become Britain's best female distance runner, breaking British and Commonwealth records at 5,000 metres, 3,000 metres, 10,000 metres and at the half marathon, she didn't win the medals for which she strove until years later. Through injury and illness Paula was forced to miss the 1994 and 1998 Commonwealth games. In the 2000 Olympic games in Sydney she just missed out on the bronze medal in the 10,000 metres. In 2002 she finally won a gold medal in the 5,000 metres at the Commonwealth Games in Manchester. Winning gold on her home soil was a truly emotional moment for Paula.

In the years 2002 and 2003 Paula hit a winning streak, especially in road running. Her record-breaking marathon wins in Chicago and London; a world cross-country title and impressive wins on road and track, have turned her into a household name. Her easy-going natural manner has added to her popularity and in 1999, 2001 and 2002 she was voted British Female Athlete of the Year. In 2002 she was awarded the MBE (Member of the Order for the British Empire) by the Queen.

Paula on her way to breaking the world record in the London Marathon, 2003

weblinks

For more information about Paula Radcliffe, go to
www.waylinks.co.uk/21CentLives/Sport

"What Paula has achieved is a quantum leap not only for women's marathon-running but the men's as well. After her achievement today, everyone should be re-thinking their game plan."
Gerard Hartmann, Paula's fitness trainer after the London Marathon, April 2003

The *Scotsman*, 14 April 2003

Roger Federer with the Wimbledon trophy

> **"** I think it was a bit hard on me to be compared to Sampras [at such a young age]. He has achieved so much in his career and I was just starting out. Maybe we are both very relaxed on court, we have the same technique and we use the same racket. We also share the same star sign but I would say we are very different players. **"**
> Roger Federer on being compared with Pete Sampras

Name: Roger Federer

Date and place of birth: 8 August 1981, Basel, Switzerland

Training: Roger became a member of a tennis club when he was eight years old. He started playing in regional tournaments and then went on to play in international games at a junior level when he was just 12. Roger was then accepted into the Swiss performance centre in Ecublens where he learnt how to perfect his tennis skills.

Major achievements: In 1998 he was seeded number one junior tennis player in the world and won the Wimbledon junior singles and doubles titles. He won his first Wimbledon Championship in 2003 and continued his success into 2004 by winning the Australian Open and his second Wimbledon title.

Some things you might not know about him: He is a keen sportsman who also enjoys golf, football and skiing. His favourite music is by the heavy rock band AC/DC and the rock star Lenny Kravitz. In July 2003 he launched his own fragrance called 'RF-RogerFederer'.

Become a pro! Roger has worked hard mentally to be where he is today. When he was junior world number one everybody expected him to become the next big champion, like Pete Sampras. He found the pressure too much and was often moody on court, breaking his racket and having tantrums. Roger has worked hard to control his temper and these days he is known for being calm. It is his natural talent and his ability to be focused on court that has helped him reach the top.

Swiss tennis player Roger Federer has been tipped for the top since he became junior number one in 1998. Many people saw his Wimbledon win in 2003 as just the beginning of a mighty tennis career.

Roger began playing tennis when he was eight years old. As a boy his tennis heroes were the German champion Boris Becker and the Swedish star Stephan Edberg. His greatest inspiration of all was the 13 times Grand Slam Championship winner, Pete Sampras. Roger has a natural flare for the game, on clay and grass courts. His talent lies in his range of shots that always keep his opponents guessing.

A year after being ranked the junior number one in the world Roger made the leap to senior tennis. In 1999 he was in the top 100 players and by 2000 he was ranked 29th in the world. By now all eyes were on him to win a major tennis tournament. He came close in 2001 when he played Pete Sampras at Wimbledon. After five exciting sets Roger finally knocked his hero out of the competition to reach the quarter-final. Unfortunately, he was beaten in the next round by the British player Tim Henman. In the same year Roger reached the quarter-final of the French Open.

The year 2002 brought Roger some major wins but still no Grand Slam title. By 2003 people were hoping for greater things from the talented young Swiss player. His moment finally came in the final at Wimbledon when he beat the Australian Mark Philippoussis. He managed to outwit the powerful Australian with skill and strength and won the match in three sets. Roger's first Wimbledon win signalled the start of a string of victories. In 2004 he won his second Grand Slam title, beating Marat Safin in the Australian Open. As the world number one player, Roger successfully defended his Wimbledon title in July that year, beating America's Andy Roddick in a thrilling four set match. Roger looks set to enjoy many years at the top of the game.

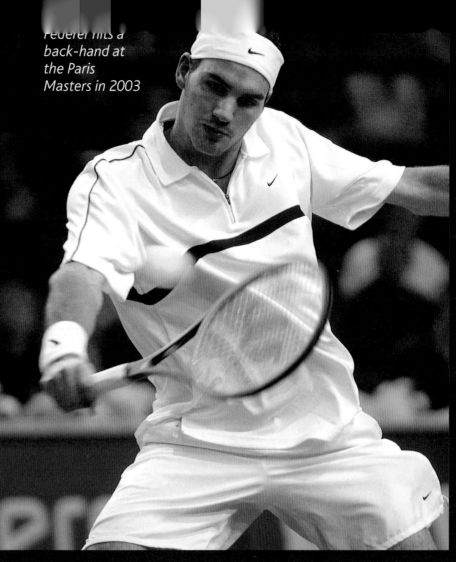

Federer hits a back-hand at the Paris Masters in 2003

"Behind [Federer's] poker face and cold exterior is an emotional young man as we saw with the scenes that followed his win. He has not played great in grand slams before but he was very convincing in the final. He is a deserved champion...I am convinced he will win many more Wimbledons and US Opens and other grand slams. The future has come today."
Three-time Wimbledon champion Boris Becker

The *Guardian*, July 2003

Weblinks!

For more information about Roger Federer, go to
www.waylinks.co.uk/21CentLives/Sport

Other Sports People

Tanni Grey–Thompson

The paralympic wheelchair racer Tanni Grey-Thompson has an impressive collection of gold medals and has done much to raise the profile of wheelchair athletes. Tanni was born in Wales in 1969 and has been in a wheelchair since she was eight. As a child she played basketball, swimming and tennis before settling on athletics as her chosen sport. She joined her first athletics club during her mid-teens. Tanni went on to study politics at Loughborough University where she was able to develop her sporting career. She entered her first Paralympics in Seoul in 1988 where she excelled in the 100 metre, 200 metre and 800 metre wheelchair races. It wasn't until the Paralympics in Sydney in 2000 that she became a household name. She won 13 Paralympic medals, including four gold medals in the 100 metre, 200 metre, 400 metre and 800 metre wheelchair races. She has been awarded the MBE and the OBE. Tanni has also collected nine medals in the London marathon and broken 20 World Records. She is an active member of the Sports Council for Wales.

Wayne Rooney

Wayne Rooney has become the English football star of his generation. The Everton striker made sporting history when he became the youngest player to score for England in the match against Macedonia in 2003. Born on 24 October 1985, Wayne was just 16 when he signed for Everton. He made his debut for the first team in the 2002/2003 season and became an overnight sensation when he scored the winning goal for Everton in the last minute of their match against Arsenal. Wayne's career has gone from strength to strength: in 2002 he was named BBC Young Sportsperson of the Year, then in 2003 he made his debut for England when he came on at half time against Australia. At 17, he had already broken records by becoming the youngest person to play for the national team. Wayne became a national hero in Euro 2004 when he scored four of England's ten goals during the tournament.

Denise Lewis

The English athlete Denise Lewis specialises in the heptathlon, an athletic event for women in which they take part in seven different events over two days. To compete in the heptathlon takes a special kind of person who can take on the 100 metre hurdles, high jump, shot put, 200 metres, long jump, javelin and 800 metres. Denise was born on 27 August 1972 in West Bromich, England. She specialised in the heptathlon early in her career, coming fifth in the European Junior Championships in 1991. At the Commonwealth Games in 1994 she won her first gold medal. She has gone on to win many medals for Britain and has broken Commonwealth records. In 1998 she overcame injuries to win the gold at the European and Commonwealth Games. She gave one of her best performances at the Sydney Olympic Games in 2000 when she won Olympic gold. She was awarded the MBE in 1999 and the OBE in 2001.

Lennox Lewis

The British heavyweight boxer Lennox Lewis was born in London, England on 2 September 1965. His mighty fighting style first caught the public eye at the 1988 Olympics when he won a gold medal for super heavyweight boxing. Soon afterwards he returned to Britain and in 1989 he turned professional. By 1990 Lennox was European Heavyweight Champion, then in 1991 he became British Heavyweight Champion. He was awarded the World Boxing Council Heavyweight Belt by default in 1993 when American World Heavyweight Champion Riddick Bowe refused to fight him. He kept the title until 1994 when he was defeated by Oliver McCall. Three years later he bounced back to reclaim the title from McCall. Then in 1999 he became undisputed World Heavyweight Champion when he beat Evander Holyfield. In 2000 he lost his title to South African boxer Hasim Rahman but regained it in the rematch. In 2002 he finally met the famous US heavyweight, Mike Tyson. The odds seemed stacked against Lennox but he knocked the American out in the eighth round. Lennox was awarded an MBE in 1998. In 2004 he became the first reigning World Heavyweight Champion to retire in nearly 50 years.

Tim Henman

The tennis player Tim Henman was born on 6 September 1974 in Oxford, England. He began playing tennis when he was two-years-old and has gone on to become the most famous British tennis player of his generation. Though he has won many international tennis titles and has been ranked as one of the top ten players in the world, he is yet to win a Grand Slam title. Each year his fans get behind him as he tries to win the Wimbledon Championship, a title Tim dreams of winning because it is played on his home soil and is still considered by many players to be the best title in the world. Tim has reached five semi-finals and one quarter final and still believes that he will lift the famous Wimbledon trophy one day.

Pippa Funnell

In the world of horses and eventing Britain's Pippa Funnell is perhaps the best in the world. In 2003 she became the first person to win the eventing Grand Slam: the Kentucky, Badminton and Burghley. At each competition Pippa performed outstandingly at dressage, the 30-fence, four-mile cross-country and in the show-jumping arena. Pippa was born on 7 October 1968 in Crowborough, UK. She has won many competitions and medals at Junior, Young Rider and Senior level. She has represented Britain at the Olympics, helping to win the Silver medal for the British eventing team at the Sydney Olympics in 2000. She went on to win the team and individual gold medals at the European Championships in 1999 and 2001. In November 2003 *The Sunday Times* newspaper voted her their Sportswoman of the Year.

Index